7 Steps to
High-Income
Freelancing

Get the clients you deserve

Lori De Milto

Dedication

To my husband Julian De Milto, who has always believed in me.

Acknowledgments

I had a lot of help in developing this book and would like to thank:

- Brian Corchiolo, visual-graphic designer/web developer, bpc Creative, who designed the book cover

- Kathleen Labonge, MBA, freelance medical copyeditor, Write Point Editing Solutions, who edited the book

- All of the freelancers who:
  - Helped me choose the title
  - Helped me choose the cover
  - Provided feedback to improve the book
  - Reviewed the book

Praise *for 7 Steps to High-Income Freelancing: Get the clients you deserve*

"The ultimate guide to freelance success! This book teaches you how to create the conditions for freelance success in seven clear, compact steps."

> Christina Bruno
> Freelance writer

"Lori's marketing guidance provided a clear path for me to find and attract my ideal clients and bypasses the usual generalities. This is a must-read for freelancers looking to attract reliable, high-paying clients."

> Lisa Baker, PhD, CMPP
> Freelance medical writer

"Lori's no-frills thesis on marketing from the University of Hard Knocks is full of practical advice that you can put to use immediately. I should know because I got my first freelance client well before I could implement all the advice in this reader-friendly book."

> Oki K. Dzivenu, DPhil, ELS
> Freelance medical writer

"*7 Steps to High-Income Freelancing* is a revelation. Using a carefully thought out, step-by-step approach, Lori De Milto artfully presents a blueprint for developing, building, and maintaining a high-income freelance business. Every chapter is targeted, precise, and succinct. She cuts no corners and she pulls no punches. If you are serious about building your freelance business, then you need this book."

> C. C. Pounds
> Freelance writer

"*7 Steps to High-Income Freelancing* gave me the knowledge and confidence to effectively grow my freelancing business. Lori shares years of experience in this easy-to-read, essential handbook that is a must-read for both novice and experienced freelance writers."

Christina Sanguinetti
Freelance medical writer

"I've been freelancing full time for six years and make a good income. But Lori De Milto's *7 Steps to High-Income Freelancing* inspires me to refocus and do even better. This wonderful little book is packed with insider tips—some of which I know from experience and a few that are brand new. Pure freelance gold!"

Genevieve J. Long, PhD
Freelance medical writer specializing
in patient and consumer education

"If you're looking for a silver bullet, this isn't one. Instead, you'll find concise and actionable steps, minus the fluff. I've read many books and guides telling me to 'choose my niche' or 'find clients on LinkedIn' but very few have actually given me a step-by-step breakdown of how to do that. *7 Steps To High-Income Freelancing* is one such book!"

Nifty Jacob
Copywriter

"Until I read *7 Steps to High-Income Freelancing*, I didn't have a clear plan for how to grow my freelance business. Now, not only do I have the tools, but I know it can be done."

Malaika I. Hill
Principal medical writer
MD Writing & Editing Solutions, LLC

"The Mighty Marketer delivers—again! Most marketing books are so broad and far-reaching they leave freelancers hopelessly discouraged. When are we supposed to get our actual work done if we have to spend so much time and energy marketing and updating all those social media accounts?

Fortunately Lori De Milto is true to her promise. She cuts through all that clutter with her targeted, realistic approach. Concentrating on her seven steps makes a freelancer's life not only easier, but also profitable. You've also got to love an entrepreneur who's not afraid to share her own mistakes. I've rewritten my marketing plan based on this book."

> Michele Hanley, BS, MPA
> Michele Hanley Copywriting

"These seven steps, based on Lori's real-life business success, provide a straightforward, practical guide to marketing for freelancers. She breaks the information down into meaningful topics, so the overall marketing process is less daunting. This is a valuable resource every freelancer should own."

> Kathleen Labonge, MBA
> Freelance medical copyeditor

"With an easy-to-read format and simple step-by-step approach, *7 Steps to High-Income Freelancing* gives excellent food for thought for any aspiring freelance writer, but information from the book can also help those who have been working in the industry for years. This book is a great guide to launch and expand your freelancing business and should be considered a 'must read' for freelancers from all walks of life!"

> Keith D'Oria
> Editor

"Freelance writers often struggle to find great clients. This book's concise, practical advice streamlines the process. I learned many of its tips the hard way; with this guide, you won't have to."

Amy Karon, DVM, MPH, MA
Freelance medical journalist

"Marketing is essential for any business and it is hard to keep up with all the activities you need to manage as a freelancer. With this book, Lori De Milto created a wonderful guide for new and experienced freelancers, with a step-by-step process and advice on how to get better clients and explain your value. I highly recommend this book!"

Rosa Fierro
Bilingual art director
Metamorpha Creative

"Every freelancer should have Lori De Milto's new book, *7 Steps to High-Income Freelancing*. With her easy-to-follow marketing plan, new and experienced freelancers alike can boost their confidence and their income."

Elizabeth Hanson
Freelance science and medical writer

"*7 Steps to High-Income Freelancing* is an essential read for freelancers. It is filled to the brim with specific marketing strategies that can be used by freelancers at all stages of their careers. Lori makes it easy to follow her tips by providing step-by-step checklists, spreadsheets, and templates—the bonus materials are fantastic! In my opinion, every single freelancer, from brand new to seasoned and successful, would benefit from reading this book."

Gail Flores, PhD
President and principal writer
Encore Biomedical Communications
Experts in Oncology

"*7 Steps to High-Income Freelancing* is filled with actionable, step-by-step marketing advice for freelancers. The book is easy to navigate and has helpful bonus content (including the direct email swipe file, which I find extremely helpful). With this one little book, my whole marketing plan is done! Every freelancer should have a copy of Lori's new book!"

"Annie" Kai Cheang, PharmD, MS
Principal medical writer
Scientific Value

"The insights in *7 Steps to High-Income Freelancing* are invaluable! After following Lori's guidance on building a compelling website, I've received compliments from many clients. This is an essential book to have for any freelancer."

Mia DeFino, MS
Freelance medical and science writer

"Lori De Milto's *7 Steps to High-Income Freelancing* is a handy guide for new freelancers and those who are having a hard time growing their business. Lori is generous in sharing her personal experiences and tricks of the trade in an easy-to-follow format."

Monica Nicosia, PhD
Freelance medical writer
Nicosia Medical Writer LLC

"I was excited to read Lori's practical book, *7 Steps to High-Income Freelancing*, and find smart advice on how to approach my freelance marketing strategy, even after 27 years of freelancing. I particularly appreciate her detailed suggestions on how to "mine" LinkedIn features to find contacts, now that Microsoft has taken over."

Elizabeth Frick, PhD, ELS
Technical and medical editor
Author of *Business Matters: A Freelancer's Guide to Business Success in Any Economy*

Table of Contents

7 Steps to
High-Income Freelancing

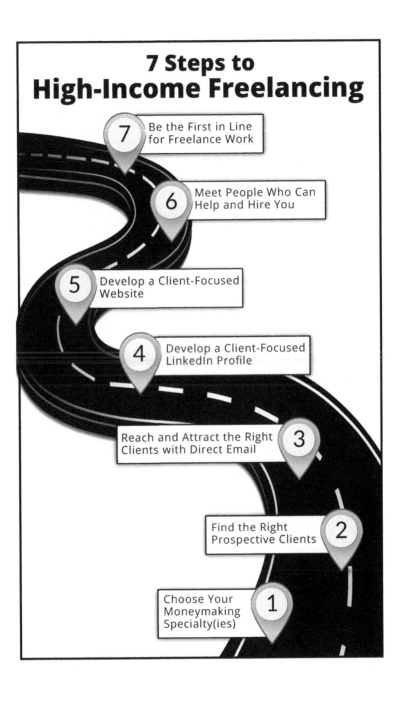

7 — Be the First in Line for Freelance Work

6 — Meet People Who Can Help and Hire You

5 — Develop a Client-Focused Website

4 — Develop a Client-Focused LinkedIn Profile

3 — Reach and Attract the Right Clients with Direct Email

2 — Find the Right Prospective Clients

1 — Choose Your Moneymaking Specialty(ies)

Introduction

"If you can dream it, you can do it."
— Walt Disney

Getting great clients is hard for most freelancers. Creating a steady, high-income freelance business is harder. But this isn't your fault.

Freelancers rarely have a chance to learn about marketing. Maybe you don't know where to start or what works best. Maybe what you've tried hasn't worked, and you don't want to waste any more time. Or maybe you hate "selling" yourself. So you end up taking whatever work comes along, instead of finding the clients you deserve.

It doesn't have to be that way.

Clients Need You

Awesome clients who need the help of talented freelancers are out there. These clients will pay you what you're worth, treat you right, and hire you again and again. In this book, I'll show you how to find, reach, and get them.

Within 18 months of starting my freelance writing business, I was a 6-figure freelancer doing work I loved for clients who treated me right. I didn't do this by being smarter than other freelancers—because I'm not. I did it by figuring out the best ways to find, reach, and get the right clients.

And I'm sharing my secrets in this book. You'll learn what works best for freelancers in getting high-paying clients, so you won't waste your time, effort, or money. And you won't be overwhelmed by all of the marketing options and advice out there—much of which doesn't work for freelancers. You'll also get bonus content to help you succeed.

Choose Freelance Success

You can sit around and hope that high-paying clients magically appear. You can continue to work with low-paying clients who don't value you, or you can use the proven process that's helped me and hundreds of other freelancers succeed. The choice is yours.

Every freelancer can become a Mighty Marketer and create a steady, high-income freelance business. This book shows you what you need to do and how to do it. If you're willing to work hard, you can start to see changes in just a few months!

Ready to get started on your journey to freelance success?

Step 1. Choose Your Moneymaking Specialty(ies)

"If you aim at nothing, you'll hit it every time."

— Zig Ziglar

Succeed by Specializing

Specializing is the fastest, easiest way to get great clients. If you have a bad leak and water is pouring onto your floor, you're going to call a plumber, not a handyman, because the plumber is an expert in solving your problem. When clients hire a freelancer, they want an expert too: someone who specializes in whatever they need help with. And they're willing to pay well for that expertise.

In Step 1, you'll learn how to:

- Find and assess freelance opportunities in different specialties
- Choose (or refine) your moneymaking specialty(ies)
- Prepare to get great clients in your specialty(ies).

If you already specialize, you'll learn how to make sure you've chosen a specialty where you can make money now and in the future—and if you haven't, how to switch your focus.

Make More Money with Less Effort

Clients are willing to pay well for freelancers who have the expertise to meet their needs. That's why specializing helps you get high-paying clients—instead of taking whatever work comes along.

Specializing also helps you get the clients you deserve with less work and in less time. By specializing, you'll learn more about your clients (your target markets). You'll know who your prospective clients (prospects) are, where to find them, what they need, and how you can meet those needs. You'll be able to show clients that you understand their needs and have the expertise to help them.

As a specialist, you'll have less competition for high-paying clients, and those clients will be able to find you more easily. Colleagues, a key source of referrals, will also be more likely to remember you—and what you do. And as a specialist, you'll build expertise and will be able to work faster and with less effort.

Choosing a specialty, or niche, and moving toward it takes time for most freelancers. Your specialty can—and usually should—change as you get more experience and learn more about the market for your services. Start more broadly and narrow down your specialty over time.

You can start with two or three specialties, and may even keep two or three specialties throughout your freelance career. Having more than one specialty helps you if one specialty stops growing.

Examples of Freelance Specialties

Let's look at my specialty as an example.

Specialty #1:
Freelance medical writer

Freelance medical writer is a specialty, but it's very broad. As I learned more about freelance medical writing, I found out that there are two basic types: marketing communications and scientific. With my background in journalism, I was definitely a marketing communications medical writer.

Specialty #2:
Freelance marketing communications medical writer

But even within medical marketing communications, there are subspecialties. As I gained more experience, learned

4

more about the marketplace, and figured out the type of work I liked best, I revised my specialty again.

> *Specialty #3:*
> Freelance medical writer for healthcare marketers and health organizations

Today, I'm a freelance medical writer who delivers targeted content for healthcare marketers and health organizations. My target markets are hospitals, large medical practices, disease-focused health organizations, communications agencies working in healthcare, and patient education organizations. This is much narrower than my first specialty.

Other Sample Freelance Specialties

- Food and nutrition consultant and writer
- Writer for university magazines and websites
- Business and financial editor
- Journal articles editor
- Website designer for small businesses
- Book cover designer

Decide How to Specialize

A moneymaking specialty:

- Offers lots of opportunities for freelancers like you now and in the future

- Makes it easy for you to find and reach prospects.

Finding your moneymaking specialty(ies) does take time and effort, but the work you put in now will help you get great clients throughout your freelance career.

Ways to Specialize

The most common ways to specialize are by industry, by project, or by a combination of industry and project.

Industry Specialization

Industry specialization means focusing on an industry, part of an industry, and/or type of client within an industry.

Example based on my specialty:

- *Industry specialty*: Medical writing
- *Part of the industry where I focus*: Healthcare services and consumer/patient education
- *Type of clients*: Hospitals, large medical practices, disease-focused health organizations, healthcare communications agencies, and patient education organizations

Project Specialization

Project specialization is based on services. This is very broad, so you'll also need to figure out what type of clients to target.

Examples:

- Writing white papers and case studies
- Editing books
- Web design

Combined Industry and Project Specialization

The narrowest specialization combines industry and project specialization.

Examples:

- Editing for authors of books
- Web design for the financial services industry

Combined industry and project specialization lets you focus on specific types of clients and services. There's less competition because your specialization is so narrow. This type of specialty generally works best if you're an experienced freelancer and you know your target market(s) really well.

The Best Way to Specialize

For most freelancers, industry specialization is best, especially if you're fairly new to freelancing or have been freelancing for a while but aren't as successful as you'd like to be. It's a broader way to specialize, and it lets you choose industries with high-paying clients.

You can do work outside your specialty(ies) too. Clients and prospects may ask you to do other types of work for them. Whether you say yes is up to you, but doing work outside your specialty(ies) is a great way to get new experience and possibly expand your specialty(ies). If you do say yes, make sure you can do a great job for the client.

Choose Your Industries and Services

Build your business faster and with less effort by starting with what you know. You can change or expand your specialty(ies) later.

Choose the clients you want to work with (your industries) and the services you provide. Focus first on the industries and types of clients and where you have the most chance of success because of your background, experience, and skills.

Examples:

If you:

- Worked full time as a writer for a Fortune 500 company, focus on large businesses

- Were a graphic designer for a university, focus on colleges and universities

- Don't have much or any work experience, focus on something related to your college degree or other training.

Prioritize your services and your industries based on your experience, expertise, and interests.

Assess Your Target Markets

Assess the target markets that interest you to make sure the industry(ies) and the type of clients offer you:

- Growing markets that need your freelance services
- Associations where you can learn about freelance opportunities, find and reach prospects, and network.

Networking with other freelancers online and in person can help you assess target markets. Look for other freelancers in professional associations in the industries that interest you, and in various groups and forums for freelancers, like:

- Freelance Success, an online community of professional, nonfiction writers
- Freelancers Union, an online community for all types of freelancers
- LinkedIn groups for freelancers and groups with members who are freelancers.

Ask them about their experiences with the target markets you're working in or considering.

Growth and Need

Choose healthy markets that are growing, like healthcare, technology, and financial services. Information about which markets are growing or shrinking is easily available online, for example, on the website of the U.S. Bureau of Labor Statistics. Follow the business media to learn more about specific industries.

Assessing a target market's overall growth potential is easier than finding out whether a target market needs your freelance services. Networking with other freelancers—online or in person—is really helpful in doing this. You can:

- Attend meetings or conferences of professional associations in your target markets

- Attend meetings or conferences of freelancers like you (e.g., a conference for freelance writers if you're a writer)

- Network online through discussion forums.

Look for freelancers working in your target industry(ies) and ask them about the freelance market. You can find these freelancers through membership directories or member lists of online communities and professional associations. Read the profiles and/or websites of other freelancers and contact some who are doing what you'd like to do.

Professional Associations

Professional associations are vital to a successful freelance business for many reasons. In choosing your specialty(ies), professional associations help you:

- Learn about target markets and stay updated on what's happening

- Easily find prospects to market to through their membership directories.

You can also build a strong network through professional associations, which will help you get more referrals (covered under Step 6. Meet People Who Can Help and Hire You).

Before joining a professional association, check out the website and available resources, and try to go to a meeting or conference. The American Medical Writers Association has played a key role in my success. I've been a member since the year after I started my business. I've joined several other associations over the years but none have been nearly as good in terms of networking and learning.

BONUS CONTENT:

The Absolute Best Way to Attract Bigger, Better Clients

Insights from Ilise Benun and proof from Ed Gandia that freelancers who specialize make more money than those who don't in this blog post

https://mightymarketer.lpages.co/bonus-content/

(NOTE: After mightymarketer, the next letter is "l" as in lion).

Describe Your Specialty(ies)

Next, describe your specialty(ies) by writing a draft summary of your specialty(ies) and listing your top services.

Write a Client-Focused Specialty Summary

Write a draft summary of your specialty(ies) based on your target clients and how you help them. You'll end up with a concise summary like this one:

> "I help [WHO YOU HELP] do [WHAT THEY WANT TO ACHIEVE], so [WHY THEY CARE ABOUT ACHIEVING IT]."

My example:

> I help hospitals, disease-focused health organizations, patient education organizations, and other health and healthcare organizations engage, inform, and motivate target audiences so:
>
> - Hospitals and health and healthcare organizations can grow their businesses
>
> - Disease-focused health organizations and patient education organizations can help more people stay healthy or live better.

10

Your summary doesn't have to be perfect. It's just for you, so you understand how to target your marketing. You'll probably use some, but not all, of the summary in your marketing.

It's okay if you don't have all of the information you need to write this type of summary yet. Write a general specialty summary for now.

Example of a general summary for my business:

> Freelance medical writer for healthcare marketers and health organizations

After you finish this book, you'll be able to add details to your client-focused specialty summary.

Your Services

Make a list of the top four services you provide or want to provide. Choose your services based on what you like to do best and the services your target clients need. If you don't know which services they need, make your best guess.

At the end of your client-focused specialty summary, list your top four services. You can provide other services too, but focusing on a few will make marketing easier and more effective.

Key Takeaways

Here's a quick summary of the key takeaways from Step 1:

- Specializing is the fastest, easiest way to get great clients. You'll understand your target markets better, know where to find clients, and have more expertise and less competition.

- Moneymaking specialties are growing, need your freelance services, and have professional associations that make it easy for you to find and reach prospects.

- Choosing and defining your specialty(ies) takes time. It's okay to have two or three specialties. And your specialty(ies) can—and usually should—change over time.

- Common ways to specialize are by industry, project, or both. Industry specialization is best for most freelancers. It's usually best to start with a broader specialty and narrow it down later.

In Step 2, you'll learn how to find great prospects within your specialty(ies). After that, you'll learn how to reach and attract them with your marketing.

Step 2. Find the Right Prospects

"Opportunities are usually disguised as hard work,
so most people don't recognize them."

— *Ann Landers*

Succeed by Choosing Your Clients

Having a clearly defined specialty(ies) makes it much easier
to find high-paying clients and to choose the prospective
clients (prospects) who are most likely to hire you.

In Step 2, you'll learn how to:

*   Choose the high-paying clients you want to work with
    (your prospects)

*   Find the right people to target within each company
    (your contacts)

*   Get the hard-to-find information you need to reach your
    contacts.

You'll learn how to use professional associations to quickly
and easily develop your prospect lists and how to prioritize
your prospects to get great clients faster.

Make a Prospect List

Develop a prospect list of about 150-200 organizations that
you'd like to work with. Choose about 30-40 prospects for
now, and add more later.

Let's start with the right type of prospects to look for:

*   Prospects most likely to hire you
*   High-paying clients.

Then we'll cover how to find them and the information you
need about each prospect.

Choose the Prospects Most Likely to Hire You

Choose clients in the industry(ies) you identified in your specialty. Here's how this works, using my specialty as an example.

My general specialty is "Freelance medical writer for healthcare marketers and health organizations." That's somewhat broad, so I need to pick certain types of clients to focus on. My specialty summary includes specific target markets: hospitals, disease-focused health organizations, and other health and healthcare organizations.

Hospitals and disease-focused health organizations are easy to find, so I focused my prospect lists on these. "Other health and healthcare organizations" is a broad term that includes organizations that I hear about and add to my prospect list and other clients that find me.

In making your list, focus first on the prospects that are most likely to hire you based on your background, experience, and skills. New freelancers, for example, aren't likely to land Apple or Mayo Clinic as clients. When I started out, I focused on smaller hospitals. As I gained more experience, I began to target—and get—larger, more prestigious hospitals, like Johns Hopkins Medicine. Expand your prospect list to other clients as you gain experience.

In general, large businesses make the best clients because they often work with multiple freelancers, understand the value we bring them, and can pay us what we're worth. But there are other types of high-paying clients too, such as foundations, some non-profit organizations, some universities, and some smaller companies. The word "company" in this book refers to any type of organization that hires freelancers.

Find High-Paying Clients

Find high-paying clients for your prospect list through:

- Professional associations
- Leading company lists (e.g., Fortune 500)
- Online directories (e.g., Medical Marketing & Media top 100 agencies)
- LinkedIn.

Do it the Easy Way

Using the member directories of professional associations is the easiest way to develop a prospect list. Member directories have all of the information you need, including the contact person for each organization and his/her email address.

If you're new to freelancing or still figuring out where to focus, professional associations will help you find prospects you might not have thought to look for on your own. General business associations can be especially useful if you're still defining your specialty(ies) or exploring different specialties.

Examples:

- American Marketing Association
- International Association of Business Communicators

Joining one or a few professional associations is a lot cheaper than the cost of the time it will take you to develop your prospect list using other research. If you don't already belong to professional associations in your target markets, join now.

Use Leading Company Lists, Online Directories, and LinkedIn

You can also research prospects using leading company lists, online directories in your industries, and LinkedIn. But this takes longer than using a professional association's member directory.

15

Use leading company lists and online directories to find companies you want to work with. Then research the right person/people to reach out to using LinkedIn.

Leading Company Lists and Online Industry Directories

Leading company lists and online directories in the industries you work in or want to work in are other sources of prospects. You'll find prospects in your industries who don't belong to your professional associations in these lists and directories.

For example, for my hospital prospect list, I used U.S. News & World Reports' list of top hospitals and top children's hospitals. In the past, I've used the National Cancer Institute's list of cancer centers to develop lists of cancer centers. I know about these lists because I know my target markets.

LinkedIn

Since Microsoft acquired LinkedIn in 2016, there have been many changes. LinkedIn was more helpful for general prospect searches before the company did away with the advanced search feature. This change limits what you can do with a free account and limits the number of searches you can do each month. A paid account with Sales Navigator does many of the things advanced search used to do, but it starts at $64.99 per month (as of August 2017).

Now, LinkedIn is best for finding contacts in the companies you know you want to work with, and for finding related prospects through the People Also Viewed section.

The regular search engine is pretty good at helping you find people, since LinkedIn's algorithm sorts results by relevance. Even if you get a lot of search results, the top ones should be relevant. Search results are also based on your connections, so the larger your network, the more results you'll get. But Boolean search (e.g., using AND, OR, and "words or phrases in quotes") isn't as effective as it was before.

In the search bar, click "Search for people with filters." On the right-hand side, you can search by:

- Your connections
- Industry
- Current company
- Location (e.g., the United States)
- Language.

To do this:

- Click on the search bar
- Click "Search for people with filters."

If you know a particular company (or companies) you want to work with, you can search for that company, and then use Keywords to find people with the right job titles.

When you find someone who is a good prospect for you, check out his/her People Also Viewed section. This is a great way to find:

- Colleagues at the same company who may be better prospects for you

- People at different, but similar, companies with the same/similar job title.

(NOTE: This is based on LinkedIn's Search feature as of August 2017.)

LinkedIn only lets you search for so many people each month. They call this the "Commercial Use Limit," but they don't say what the limit is. So do your most important searches first, and know that you can do more searches after the first of the next month.

Find the Right Information

Put your list in a spreadsheet, database, or even a Word file. Whatever works for you is fine.

For each client, include:

- Company
- Contact person
- Title
- Department
- Email address

If you find more than one contact person, include the name, title, department, and email address for each.

Find the Right Contact Person

Look for the types of people who usually hire freelancers, or manage the people who hire freelancers. These are usually:

- Vice presidents
- Managers
- Directors
- Associate directors
- Editors.

The right contact person usually works in departments like:

- Communications
- Content marketing
- Digital marketing
- Marketing
- New business development
- Sales
- Web content.

The titles and departments vary in different companies. As you learn more about your target market(s), you'll learn the best search terms.

Finding the right contact person or people isn't always easy. But if you get close to the right person, and send a professsional, client-focused direct email (Step 3), people will forward your message to their colleagues. This has happened to me lots of times.

It's good to have several contact people from each company, because sometimes it's difficult to find the right person. Having several contacts is especially helpful for larger companies where multiple departments may use freelancers or you're not sure which person hires freelancers.

Find the Email Address

Email addresses are difficult to find, unless you're using a professional association member directory. But I've found a trick that usually works. Find the email format for email addresses on the organization's website.

Examples:

firstinitiallastname@client.org
firstname.lastname@client.org

Try the Newsroom, which always lists media contacts, usually by name and with an actual email address. Then apply that email format to your contact's name. You can also use an automated service like pipl (https://pipl.com) to find email addresses or see if the one you found is right, but you need to start with an educated guess.

Prioritize Your Prospects

Divide your prospects into three groups:

- **Hot prospects:**
  - o Companies you most want to work with, which are often the top companies in the industry.

- **Routine prospects:**
  - o Companies you'd like to work with. These are good companies that are often smaller and less well known than the top companies in the industry.

- **Lukewarm prospects:**
  - o Companies you don't really want to work with but will for now to get some experience, make some money, etc. These are often smaller, less impressive companies.

19

Where you focus most of your marketing depends on the stage of your business:

- **New freelancer:**
  - ○ Focus mostly on lukewarm and routine prospects, which are easier to get than hot prospects.

- **Experienced freelancer who wants to be a lot more successful:**
  - ○ Focus mostly on lukewarm and routine prospects, which are easier to get.
  - ○ If you're putting lots of time into your marketing, try some hot prospects too.

- **Seasoned, successful freelancer looking for a "tune-up" (new opportunities and/or better clients):**
  - ○ Focus mostly on hot prospects.

BONUS CONTENT:

Prospect List Template

An easy way to store your prospect list and schedule and track your contact with prospects

https://mightymarketer.lpages.co/bonus-content/

Become an Expert

Making a prospect list also helps you learn more about your target market(s) and specific clients. This will help you develop the client-focused marketing that attracts high-paying clients.

As you work on your list and visit prospects' websites, make notes about the challenges they face, the language they use, and their values. Pick a few companies on your prospect list that you'd really like to work with and spend some extra time visiting their websites and taking notes.

Doing this research will help you learn what's important to your prospects and what they need. This will help you figure out what to say to get their attention and show that you can meet their needs when you reach out to them.

When I developed my list of hospitals, for example, I found that I had to use different messages to appeal to regular hospitals and children's hospitals. All hospitals have the same basic need: to get more business, which means attracting more patients.

While my marketing for regular hospitals focused on the business need of attracting more patients, my marketing for children's hospitals was softer and focused on helping them give more sick kids the best care available. I picked up the need for a different approach with children's hospitals through my research.

Key Takeaways

Here's a quick summary of the key takeaways from Step 2:

- Choose high-paying clients in the industry(ies) you identified in your specialty, and focus first on prospects that are most likely to hire you based on your background, experience, and skills. Expand your list to other clients later.

- Large businesses are often the best clients. They usually work with multiple freelancers, understand the value we bring them, and can pay us what we're worth.

- Professional associations, through their member directories, are the easiest way to develop a prospect list of high-paying clients. You can also find prospects through leading company lists, online directories, and LinkedIn.

- Making a prospect list helps you attract high-paying clients because you become an expert who understands their needs.

- Where you focus depends on whether you're a new or experienced freelancer and the type of new business you're looking for. If you're new, getting experience is the main goal. If you've got great experience, you can focus on the more prestigious companies you most want to work with.

In Step 3, you'll use your specialty(ies) and your prospect list to reach and attract the right clients.

Step 3. Reach and Attract the Right Clients with Direct Email

"The truth is that nobody cares about you—
they care about what you can do for them."

— *Melonie Dodaro*

Succeed by Being Direct

When done right, direct email is very effective in attracting high-paying clients. By carefully targeting clients who can pay you what you're worth and focusing your direct email on their needs, you make yourself irresistible to them.

In Step 3, you'll learn how to:

- Use what you've learned in working on your specialty and prospect list to show you understand client needs

- Write direct emails that prospects will read

- Start to build relationships with prospects and turn them into clients.

Understand Direct Email and Target Markets

Email marketing isn't direct email. An email that makes the same offer to thousands of people is email marketing. It may address you by name, but it's not customized to your needs. Often, email marketing isn't even relevant.

Direct email is very different. Each direct email is carefully customized to the prospect. You'll focus on what you can do for that prospect and:

- Show that you understand the prospect's needs

- Use language and values from the prospect's website

- Briefly highlight how your expertise and experience can help the prospect.

Know Your Target Markets

Clients have general, freelancer-specific, and industry- or company-specific needs.

General Needs

Common general needs are:

- Get more business (usually by selling more products or services)
- Make more money (also by selling more products or services, but the language you'll use in your direct email will be different)
- Help their clients build their businesses
- Be seen as a thought leader
- Educate and inform people
- Stay on budget and on deadline.

Freelancer-Specific Needs

When hiring a freelancer, clients need someone with excellent technical skills (writing, editing, design, etc.), along with:

- Experience in the type of work they're looking for help with
- Ability to meet deadlines (the key to repeat business)
- Excellent communication skills
- Flexibility, accessibility, and responsiveness
- Ability to take ownership of the project.

Industry- or Company-Specific Needs

Understanding the needs of an industry usually takes time. If you don't already know your industry(ies) really well, do some research through your professional associations, industry news, etc. Always stay updated on what's happening in your industry(ies).

Learning about the needs of each company isn't hard or time consuming. Just spend a few minutes on the prospect's website. The "Home" and "About" pages usually have all of the information you need. You may also want to skim through the latest annual report (a good place to identify needs). Make notes about the prospect's mission/vision/values and needs, and the key language used.

Sometimes you can use the same industry need in all direct emails to a specific type of client, with a little customization to the specific client. For example, hospitals, one of my target markets, need to get more business (patients), but face intense competition from other hospitals. I use this basic need in all of my direct emails to hospitals, and customize the language I use for each hospital based on its website.

My little trick for finding email addresses from Step 2 will come in handy when you get ready to send direct emails. If you don't have your contact's email address, find the email format (e.g., firstinitiallastname@client.org or firstname.lastname@client.org) on the company's website (Newsroom page), and apply it to your contact's name.

If you're not sure who hires freelancers, that's okay. As long as you get close to the right person and send a compelling direct email, the person is very likely to forward your direct email to colleagues. This has happened to me lots of times.

Attract Clients with Compelling Copy

Direct email needs to be very focused. What you'll write to one type of client within one industry will be very different than what you'll write to another type of client in the same industry. For example, in financial services, direct email to a bank will be different than direct email to financial advisors. In my field, medical writing, direct email to medical communications companies is very different than direct email to hospitals.

Writing the first direct email for each type of client does take time. But if you're targeting other similar companies, you can use this as a template that you can modify for each prospect in a few minutes.

Write Compelling Direct Email Copy

A targeted, compelling direct email:

- Entices with a great subject line

- Is concise and to the point, no more than six sentences

- Uses short, easy-to-read paragraphs and the right tone for the prospect

- Uses the contact's name and the company's name

- Uses a subhead for a key message related to the prospect's needs

- Encourages the contact to connect with you with a clear call to action

- Makes it easy for the person to contact you

- Uses your logo and tagline, or a brief company description, in your email signature.

BONUS CONTENT:

Direct Email Swipe File

Proven templates and examples of direct emails to help you get better, higher-paying clients

https://mightymarketer.lpages.co/bonus-content/

Spend extra time and effort on your subject line. If it's not interesting, your contact will never even open your email. In the first sentence after the greeting, clearly show that you understand the prospect's needs by combining your general knowledge of the target market with language from the company's website.

Keep your email short and to the point, no more than six sentences. After the greeting and first sentence, include one or two sentences about your relevant experience and a link to your website. If you don't have a website yet, include a link to your LinkedIn profile.

If you're a new freelancer, focus on whatever relevant experience you have and your abilities. For example, if you're a doctor transitioning into medical writing, highlight the deep knowledge of medicine your clinical experience gives you. If you're a recent college graduate, highlight relevant class projects, internships, etc.

Personalize your email by including the contact's name and the company's name. Use a subhead for a key message related to the company's needs.

Now that you've gotten the contact interested in your services, make it easy for him/her to learn more about you by including a link to your website or LinkedIn profile. Encourage a discussion or other further contact with a clear call to action and your contact information. A call to action says what you want your prospect to do next.

End the email with impact by using your logo and tagline in your email signature. If you don't have a logo and tagline yet, include a brief description of your business in your email signature.

Increase Responses by Following Up

Most positive responses to direct email come from follow-up emails. If you don't hear back from the contact in about a week, follow up. People are really busy. Sometimes they miss an email, or mean to respond but don't get to it.

Also keep everyone who hasn't said they don't use free-lancers or don't want to hire you on your targeted follow-up list, because up to 90% of the time, prospects aren't ready to hire a freelancer when you first contact them, according to Ed Gandia, a business coach and strategist who works with freelance writers and copywriters.

Many freelancers miss getting great clients because they never or rarely follow up. We'll cover this more in Step 7. Be First in Line for Freelance Work.

Follow-Up Email

The follow-up email is super easy. Just forward your original email with a short, polite follow-up email.

Plan Your Campaign

While direct email is effective, it usually takes time and follow-up to get high-paying clients. Start with the prospects that are most likely to hire you based on where you are in your freelance career:

- **New freelancer:**
  - ○ Focus mostly on lukewarm and routine prospects, which are easier to get.

- **Experienced freelancer who wants to be a lot more successful:**
  - ○ Focus mostly on lukewarm and routine prospects, which are easier to get. If you're putting lots of time into your marketing, try some hot prospects too.

- **Seasoned, successful freelancer looking for a "tune-up" (new opportunities and/or better clients):**
  - ○ Focus mostly on hot prospects.

Key Takeaways

Here's a quick summary of the key takeaways from Step 3:

- Direct email, when customized to each prospect and focused on client needs, is very effective in getting high-paying clients.

- Effective direct emails have a compelling subject line and are concise, easy to read, and personalized.

- It doesn't matter if you're not sure who hires freelancers. If you write an effective direct email, your contact will forward it to the right person.

- Most responses come from follow-up emails, sent about a week after the original email.

In Steps 4 and 5, you'll learn how to develop a strong online presence so that clients who get your direct emails will be impressed when they check you out. Step 4 covers your LinkedIn profile and Step 5 covers your website.

Step 4. Develop a Client-Focused LinkedIn Profile

"If your LinkedIn profile doesn't showcase your skills and portray you as a polished professional you are letting the ultimate opportunity just slip away..."

— Donna Serdula

Succeed by Impressing Clients on LinkedIn

Clients expect to be able to check out freelancers before contacting us about a project, and colleagues want to know we're professional before they refer work to us. To get high-paying clients, you must have a strong online presence: Your LinkedIn profile and your website.

In Step 4, you'll learn how to:

- Develop a client-focused LinkedIn profile
- Write a compelling headline and summary, the keys to attracting high-paying clients
- Use the "magic" words that will help clients find you.

You'll be able to use much or all of the work you put into your LinkedIn profile on your website (covered in Step 5). You can also use this content in professional association member profiles and freelance directories and in online forum bios.

Develop a Compelling, Client-Focused Profile

LinkedIn is the #1 social network for freelancers. In early 2017, LinkedIn revamped its interface and made major changes to the format and content of profiles. So even if you had a compelling, client-focused profile before, you need to make sure it's still effective.

The key to an effective LinkedIn profile—and all of your marketing—is to focus on client needs and how you meet those needs. A compelling, client-focused profile will help you attract clients and impress colleagues, who are a key source of referrals.

The Keys to Attracting High-Paying Clients

Put extra time and effort into your headline and summary because these are the most important parts of your LinkedIn profile. Use information from your specialty summary (from Step 1) when you write your headline and summary.

Headline

You have up to 120 characters for your headline. Use them to attract clients and impress colleagues, and make them want to learn more about you:

- Clearly say what you do and how you help your clients.

- Use the "magic" words that will make it easy for clients to find you in searches in your headline and summary:
  - "freelancer" or "freelance [YOUR FIELD HERE]"

- Use other keywords that people use to search for freelancers like you, like keywords about:
  - The type of clients you work with, e.g., financial services, medical writing, or small businesses
  - Your services, e.g., web content, academic editing, or digital design.

DULL AND COMPELLING LINKEDIN HEADLINES

Dull:

> Lori De Milto
> President at LDM Company

Compelling:

> Lori De Milto
> Freelance medical writer of targeted content, on time, every time

Dull:

> Bob Smith
> Independent business owner

Compelling:

> Bob Smith
> Freelance writer specializing in helping financial services companies attract and retain customers and clients

Dull:

> Jane Jones
> Editor

Compelling:

> Jane Jones
> Freelance editor, delivering clear, accurate content to help small businesses succeed

Summary

Only the first 201 characters (45 in mobile) in your summary show before people need to click "See more." Make sure the first two sentences of your summary flow with your headline and offer a clear, concise message. The first two sentences should be about 201 characters (it's fine for your second sentence to continue after "See more").

DULL AND COMPELLING LINKEDIN SUMMARIES: FIRST 2 SENTENCES

Dull:

> I'm actively seeking clients who need someone to write their medical documents. I work on . . .

Compelling:

> Count on me for medical content that engages your target audiences. I help healthcare marketers and health organizations effectively communicate with patients, providers, and other audiences. *(192 characters)*

Dull:

> I own MyLastName Company. I have skills that are rare among freelance writers and am passionate about my work. . .

Compelling:

> Irresistible content helps businesses attract more clients and customers. As a freelance copywriter, I write attention-grabbing websites, blogs, and other online content to help you build your business. *(196 characters)*

Dull:

> I have been working as a freelance editor since November 2014. I enjoy editing . . .

Compelling:

> As a freelance editor who specializes in working with small businesses, I deliver clear, accurate content that will help you impress your clients and customers— without spending a fortune. *(189 characters)*

Include Just Enough Key Content

Focus the rest of your summary on how you help your clients meet their needs. Include just enough key content so that clients know that you're the right choice for them, and colleagues know that you're the right freelancer to refer work to. Include a call to action, described on the next page.

Be Brief and Interesting

"Just enough" key content is a brief summary of your relevant experience, background, services, and education. Your LinkedIn profile is a marketing tool, not a resume. Make it interesting and easy to read (conversational). Throughout your profile, use:

- Short, action-oriented sentences
- Short paragraphs
- Subheads (in all caps)
- Bulleted lists.

Make a Great First Impression

Along with a compelling headline and summary, make sure your profile has the key content needed to make a great first impression and let people easily contact you:

- Professional photo
- Clear call to action
- Contact information
- Strategic keywords
- Link to your website (or samples).

Professional Photo
Show that you're professional by using a professional profile photo. You can also use your photo on your website and for other marketing.

Profile photos are now in the center of the intro section, and they're smaller and round. The ideal profile photo size, says LinkedIn, is 400 x 400 pixels. If you posted your photo before January 2017, check it and make sure it still looks right, and that key parts of the photo (like the top of your head) haven't been cropped out by the new format.

Clear Call to Action

Tell prospects what you want them to do with a call to action in your summary. Your call to action starts with a phrase or sentence that urges the prospect to take action now, like:

> Contact me today.

The best calls to action include a phrase or sentence that offers a benefit for taking action. For example, I focus on giving my clients targeted medical content, so my call to action says:

> Find Out How Targeted Medical Content Can Help You.

After your benefit phrase or sentence, include your contact information and your website's URL.

Contact Information

Make it easy for prospects and colleagues to contact you by including your email address, and, if you're comfortable, your phone number:

- Under "Contact and Personal Info" (now to the right of your headline)
- Near the end of your summary.

This is basic, but people often forget to do this. Include your website URL under "Contact and Personal Info," too, so people can easily learn more about you.

Strategic Keywords

Using the right keywords in your headline will help more clients find you when they search for a freelancer (covered earlier in this chapter under "The Keys to Attracting High-Paying Clients"). But since LinkedIn's 2017 changes, keywords in the rest of your profile aren't as important to search results as they used to be.

Searches are now influenced more by:

- Your activity (sharing and engaging) and your network, which we'll cover in Step 6
- Things you have in common with the people searching for you
- Skills listed, especially when the people searching for you have matching skills
- Profile views.

Even if keywords don't help more clients find you, they're still important in your summary to persuade the clients who do find you that you're the right freelancer for them. Include keywords about:

- Freelancing
- The type of freelancing you do
- The type of clients you work with
- Your services
- Your projects.

More people will find you if you include your industry. Even though this no longer shows on your profile, it's still there in the background, and part of LinkedIn's search algorithm. Click on the icon to edit your profile, and you'll see "Industry" between "Locations within this area" and "Summary."

Link to Your Website or Samples
Clients want to see samples of your work, or at least descriptions of what you've done, before they contact you. Include a link to your website under "Contact and Personal Info" and in your summary's call to action. If you don't have a website yet, include samples on your profile page.

BONUS CONTENT:
LinkedIn Profile Checklist for Freelancers
Create a client-focused LinkedIn profile by following this checklist.
https://mightymarketer.lpages.co/bonus-content/

Get it Right

Proofread your profile carefully to make sure you've developed a client-focused, error-free profile. Check your profile on mobile apps and computers, since 60% of users now access LinkedIn on smart phones or tablets. Make sure your profile looks great on smart phones, tablets, laptops, and desktops.

Key Takeaways

Here's a quick summary of the key takeaways from Step 4:

- LinkedIn is the #1 social network for business. You need to be on it, and you need to have a client-focused profile.

- The keys to attracting high-paying clients on LinkedIn are a compelling headline and summary.

- A client-focused profile puts the needs of your clients first and explains how you meet their needs.

- Your LinkedIn profile isn't a resume:
  - Include just enough key content—and the right content—so that clients know that you're the right choice for them.
  - Be interesting and conversational.

In Step 5, you'll learn about the other key part of your online presence: your website. Step 6, on networking, will cover how to build your LinkedIn network and use it effectively.

Step 5. Develop a Client-Focused Website

"Marketing is a contest for people's attention."
— *Seth Godin*

Succeed by Impressing Clients with Your Website

Just as clients expect freelancers to be on LinkedIn, they expect us to have websites too. A compelling, client-focused website shows clients that you're the right choice for them and colleagues that you're a professional who will do a great job if they refer work to you.

Most of the advice that's out there about websites for small businesses doesn't work for freelancers, and some of it can actually damage your reputation. Step 5 highlights how to develop a freelance website that's just right to attract high-paying clients.

In Step 5, you'll learn how to:

• Identify the essential web pages for freelancers
• Develop web content that attracts clients and colleagues
• Choose a website design that helps you communicate effectively
• Avoid common pitfalls in freelance websites.

Develop a Compelling, Client-Focused Website

A website is a key part of marketing any business today—and freelancers are running businesses. Your website needs two things:

1. Content that's compelling, clear, and focused on client needs
2. Design that's clean and clear.

38

That's it. A great website for a freelancer isn't complex or lengthy. And if you've already developed a client-focused LinkedIn profile, you'll have much of the information you need for your web content.

Pre-Sell and Pre-Qualify Clients

Done right, your website will:

- Impress high-paying clients and colleagues by showing them you understand client needs

- Highlight your expertise, skills, and work (usually with samples)

- Show that you're a professional who is running a business.

Your website pre-sells and pre-qualifies clients. When clients contact you, they'll already know a lot about you and your services. So you won't have to work as hard to convince them to hire you. And because clients know more about you, you'll get fewer emails and phone calls about work that you don't do. Your website also helps colleagues decide if you're the right freelancer for a referral.

Include the Essential Web Pages

These are the essential web pages for freelancers:

- Home
- About
- Services*
- Portfolio, Samples, or Work*
- Testimonials, Clients, or Testimonials and Clients*
- Contact.

You can combine and organize "Services"; "Portfolio, Samples, or Work"; and "Testimonials," "Clients," or "Testimonials and Clients" in different ways, covered later in this chapter.

Home

The "Home" page sets the tone and personality of your website. It's the most important page, because if clients and colleagues don't like what they see, they won't click further or contact you. You'll write this last, so we'll cover it in more detail after the other essential web pages.

About

You can call this "About," "About [your first and last name]," "About [first name]," "About [company name]," or "About Me." Including a photo helps clients see that you and your services are real. Most good freelancers' websites I've seen put the photo on the "About" page. Some freelancers put the photo on their "Home" page, which can work too. Use a professional headshot.

Start the "About" page with one or two sentences of client-focused marketing content about why the prospect should use your services. Then include the information that's most relevant to clients about your experience, education, awards and honors, and other professional accomplishments.

But this is not a resume. Some of the information is the same, but you'll present it in a more interesting, less detailed way. Using subheads like experience and education, with bullets for the relevant information, is a great way to provide this content. You can include a link to your resume or a longer bio if you want to provide complete details.

3 Pages: Many Ways to Organize

As mentioned, "Services"; "Portfolio, Samples, or Work"; and "Testimonials," "Clients," or "Testimonials and Clients" can be combined and organized in different ways. How you do this depends partly on your experience and partly on your preferences.

The page descriptions here focus on separate pages, but you should do whatever works best for your circumstances. If you're just starting out, for example, you won't have pages for testimonials and clients. That's okay. If you only have one or two testimonials, that's not enough for a separate page, but one or two testimonials will work great as part of other pages.

Here are a few ideas for organizing these pages:

- Put services and samples on one page. This works well if you don't have a lot of samples yet. If your samples are proprietary and you can't share them, include services and a project list, covered later in this chapter.

- Use one or two testimonials on the services page if you only have one or two testimonials.

- Put testimonials on your samples page.

- Sprinkle testimonials throughout your website.

- Put all testimonials on a testimonials page.

Services

Ways to categorize "Services" include:

- Services
- Projects
- Areas of expertise or topic areas.

Simple bulleted lists work great here. The categories you use depend on the type of work you do. Sample categories could include:

- Services (e.g., writing, editing, consulting, publication management, and training)

- Projects (e.g., journal articles, continuing medical education, white papers, newsletters, web content, blogs, and social media)

- Areas of expertise, topic areas, or therapeutic areas (e.g., cardiovascular disease, cancer, diabetes, and financial planning).

Portfolio, Samples, or Work

Samples of your work are a great marketing tool and something most clients expect to see. Use categories to make it easy for them to find what they're most interested in—and to highlight the type of work you most want to do. The exact categories depend on the type of work you do. For example, I like writing for patients and consumers best, so I made that my first category.

If You Don't Have or Can't Share Samples

If you're a new freelancer and don't have client samples or enough client samples, or your work is proprietary and you can't share it, don't worry. There are ways to get samples. And you can also use project lists and descriptions to show what you've done and can do.

Here are some great ways to get samples:

- Your website content
- LinkedIn articles (see Step 6)
- Volunteer work for professional organizations
- School projects
- Spec samples (a speculative sample that's like a project you want to work on).

If Your Work is Proprietary

If you can't share samples because your work is proprietary, call the web page something like "My Work" instead of "Portfolio" or "Samples." Then use a project list and/or brief project descriptions to show what you've done.

A brief project description for proprietary work could be something like this:

"Wrote a slide deck on a diabetes drug for a pharmaceutical company" *instead of:*

"Wrote a slide deck on ABC drug for XYZ Pharmaceutical Company"

Project Descriptions

Project descriptions also let you provide more information about your samples, including the companies you've worked with and your role on the project. If you have prestigious clients, naming them helps boost your credibility. If your clients aren't well known, the project descriptions explain who they are and what they do.

Project descriptions are especially helpful when you've used skills beyond your normal freelance work. For example, if you're a writer but you helped the client develop a newsletter, that's a skill you can highlight in the project description.

SAMPLE PROJECT DESCRIPTION

Format:

> Title of project
> Description of project and client
> My role (if desired)
> Link to sample (if you can share it)

Example:

> "Pregnant Mother Survives Massive Blood Loss"
>
> *Breakthroughs* patient and consumer magazine, for Robert Wood Johnson University Hospital, a leading academic medical center (New Brunswick, N.J.)
>
> My role: Conducted research, interviewed patient and physician, and wrote story.
>
> Sample

43

Testimonials

What others say about you is far more powerful than what you say about yourself. Testimonials from satisfied clients help you attract more clients—because new clients want to know that other clients found your services valuable. Testimonials are the business version of social proof that's everywhere these days in reviews of products and services and on social media.

You can combine "Testimonials" with "Clients" on one page, have two separate pages, or sprinkle testimonials throughout your website. If you're a new freelancer, you won't have this page/these pages yet. That's fine. Add "Testimonials" and "Clients" when you're ready.

You can ask any client who's happy with your work for a testimonial, but I think it's best to ask clients you've worked with for a while. A great time to ask for a testimonial is when a client compliments you during or after a project.

Explain how you'll use the testimonial, and that you'll send it to the person for final approval before posting. If you already have some testimonials, send along an example.

When someone sends you a testimonial, do any editing necessary to correct mistakes or to shorten a very long testimonial. Then add the identifying information you plan to use below the testimonial (e.g., client's name and organization, and perhaps the location). Email this to the client asking for final approval. Never use anything that someone has said about you without asking for permission first.

Clients

The "Clients" section or page is easy to develop. Choose categories that let you highlight your most important services and interests, such as industries or types of work. Or just list your clients. Using a partial list of clients, labeled "Sample Clients" or "Select Clients" is a good idea.

Include a brief description, because other clients may not know your clients. Or they may recognize the name but not know how impressive your clients are.

For example, some of my client descriptions are:

"one of the nation's leading academic medical centers"

"the nation's largest health and healthcare foundation."

On my website, I include a sample client list below the testimonials, with a brief description of each client and a link to the organization's website. (If you have the paperback, the URL is: www.writerforrent.net.)

Contact

Make it easy for people to contact you with a simple "Contact" page. Include your name, email address, and phone number. I recommend that you also include your city and state, to help show that you're running a real business.

Start your "Contact" page with a call to action (what you want the client to do). This can be something as simple as "Learn more about how I can help you."

Don't use a contact form. Your goal is to build relationships with prospects, and contact forms are distant and annoying. Plus, when a prospect decides to hire or consider you, he/she almost always wants to reach you fast. Contact forms may be necessary for corporations and other big organizations, but they're never appropriate for, or helpful to, freelancers.

Home Page

Now we're back to your "Home" page. While your "Home" page should be short, what you say here — and how your "Home" page looks — is crucial. If it's not clear and compelling, prospects won't click further—or hire you.

Using information from your specialty summary (from Step 1), concisely describe what you do and who you do it for.

Make sure your tone and language will appeal to your target clients.

After you draft your home page, go back to the rest of your content and make any necessary revisions to reinforce your key messages and language. Include your email address and phone number at the bottom of your "Home" page and every page of your website.

Write Clear, Compelling Web Content

Writing web content is very different than other types of writing. According to the Nielsen Norman Group, web users:

- Scan, reading only 20% to 28% of the average web page
- Stay on an average web page less than a minute
- Often stay on a web page 10 seconds or less.

So if clients don't find what they need on your website fast, they'll leave—and move on to the next freelancer on their list. Draw clients into your website and keep them there long enough to do what you want them to do through compelling web content. Focus on client needs and how you help them meet their needs.

Be Conversational and Concise

Make your content more personal and inviting by writing like you're having a conversation with someone. Focus on the benefits you offer clients. Use attention-grabbing headlines and subheads to convey key messages fast. Put the most important information first.

Chunk Content

Break up (or chunk) information into topics and subtopics. Use headings and subheads to:

- Draw prospects in
- Help prospects quickly find information
- Make scanning easier.

Engage Users

Keep paragraphs short and sentences simple. On the web, a one-sentence paragraph is fine. Use simple, familiar words that your target clients understand. Avoid jargon, and avoid or limit confusing acronyms and abbreviations. Make your content easier to understand and more powerful by using the active voice and lots of verbs.

Emphasize Key Points

Use bulleted lists, where appropriate, to make content easier to read. Use numbered lists if your content has instructions and/or steps.

BONUS CONTENT:

Freelance Website Checklist

Create a client-focused website by following this checklist.

https://mightymarketer.lpages.co/bonus-content/

Communicate Effectively with a Clean, Clear Design

Your website design must be visually engaging and professional, and clearly communicate your key messages. Some elements of compelling web content also contribute to effective web design, like lots of headlines and subheads. Other key design elements are:

- Choosing fonts that are easy to read online
- Choosing colors that create balance and harmony, and make reading online easy
- Putting the most important information where people are most likely to read it: the top and left part of the screen

- Making sure that everything loads quickly so you don't lose people
- Optimizing the design for mobile devices so that your website looks great on computers, tablets, and smart phones.

Hire a Designer or Do-It-Yourself?

For many freelancers, developing an effective web design requires hiring a professional web designer. The other way to develop a website is to do it yourself using a drag-and-drop website builder like Squarespace, Weebly, or Wix.

I've visited the websites of thousands of freelancers and unfortunately, most are missing the essential web content and clean, clear design that attracts high-paying clients. If you decide to do-it-yourself, make sure you can do a professional job.

Why Hire a Web Designer?

When you hire a great web designer, you know that your website will be professional. It will cost you more than developing your website yourself, but having a website that attracts clients, instead of driving them away, is well worth the investment. And if you're like me, and don't have strong tech skills, you won't have to deal with the frustration of trying to figure out how to do what you need to do on your own.

If the web designer develops your website on a content management platform like WordPress or a drag-and-drop website builder, once it's live, you can easily update and revise it on your own.

When choosing a web designer:

- Get recommendations from other freelancers with great websites
- Ask to see other samples of the designer's work.

Why Do It Yourself?

If you know how to choose a template that's appropriate for a freelance business, have a decent design sense, and have lots of time to spend on developing a clean, clear design, then you can do it yourself.

But be aware that templates that work for other small businesses may not work for a freelance business. And some best practices for small business websites aren't appropriate for a freelance business. For example:

- Use images on your "Home" page only if they contribute to your key messages
- You don't need a blog
- Don't use a contact form.

I explain each of these later in this chapter, under "Avoid Common Pitfalls in Freelance Websites."

Templates make it very easy for you to change things like colors and fonts, but if you don't understand good design, your website will look like it was done by an amateur.

Keep in mind that if you spend a lot more time on the design than a website designer would, you could actually be losing money by developing your own website—because that's time you could be spending on client work.

My Choice

I hired a web designer to develop my website, which is on WordPress (if you have the paperback, the URL is: www.writerforrent.net). I gave him the content in a Word document along with some notes about the design and my logo. The notes included the colors I wanted to use and links to websites I liked.

Since the website went live, I've managed about 95% of it myself. Occasionally, something comes up that I ask my designer to do for me. I could probably do most of this myself, but it's cheaper to pay him than to waste time trying to figure out how to do it myself. It's also less frustrating for me to let him take care of these things.

But drag-and-drop website builders weren't around when I developed my website. If I were developing a new freelance website today, I might try a drag-and-drop website builder. But I've had some design experience and know what should and should not be part of a freelancer's website.

Avoid Common Pitfalls in Freelance Websites

Web designers and web gurus push everyone to use images on the "Home" page, have a blog, use a contact form, and focus on search engine optimization (SEO). While these things are crucial for many types of businesses and organizations, none of them are necessary for freelancers. Some of them are actually harmful.

"Home" Page Image(s)

You can have one or more images on your "Home" page, but you don't need images. If an image doesn't contribute to your message, it doesn't belong on your "Home" page—or anywhere on your website. It will just confuse clients and colleagues and distract them from your key messages.

Don't let a web designer convince you that you need images, or add images yourself because the "Home" page template has a space for them. Don't use images because you see them on other freelancers' websites, because many of these websites aren't designed to attract high-paying clients.

A logo is one type of image that does belong on your "Home" page, if you have one, and on every page of your website. My logo is the only image on my "Home" page (if you have the paperback the URL is: www.writerforrent.net).

A logo is a symbol or other design that helps you visually convey your message and services. Combined with a tagline

(a memorable phrase or sentence that captures the essence
of your business), it's a powerful marketing tool that will set
you apart from most other freelancers. If you don't have a
logo and want one, your web designer should be able to help
you develop one or refer you to a designer who specializes in
logo design.

Blog

A key purpose of a blog is to continually provide fresh web
content and increase rankings in search results. But clients
won't be searching the web for you so you don't need to
worry about search results. And they aren't likely to read
your blog.

Many freelancers start a blog, write a few posts, and then
ignore it. Imagine a client who does see your blog and finds a
few posts from a year ago. That client will quickly move on to
the next freelancer.

A blog just isn't worth the time and effort that's necessary to
do it right, unless blogging is a major part of your freelance
business.

Contact Form

Yes, I'm repeating myself here, because this is so important.
Web designers almost always insist on a contact form. Just
say no!

A contact form is impersonal and implies that someone will
get back to you eventually. When a client decides to hire or
consider you, he/she almost always wants to reach you fast.
As freelancers, we need to build relationships with clients,
not annoy them.

Contact forms may be necessary for corporations and other
big organizations, but they're never appropriate for, or
helpful to, freelancers.

SEO

Don't worry about SEO, which involves writing web content that search engine algorithms will find and rank highly in search results. The goal of SEO is to increase the number of visitors to a website.

But clients rarely, if ever, search the web for freelancers. If they did, they'd get so many results that they'd never wade through them. Clients who want to do a general search for freelancers will use LinkedIn, a professional association directory, or a forum for freelancers.

As freelancers, we need to drive traffic to our websites through our other marketing. Your website is there to close the deal or persuade the client to contact you after you've "met" through direct email, in person, or online, or someone referred the client to you. In my view, there's no reason to spend any time, effort, or money on SEO.

Use Your Website to Market Your Business

Put your URL on all marketing materials, including your email signature, LinkedIn profile, and business cards. Including your website on your LinkedIn profile is very effective because someone who is reading your profile is just one click away from your website.

Updates

Once your website is live, you won't need to spend much time or effort maintaining it. Review your website at least quarterly and make any necessary updates. Add new samples or project descriptions. Update anything that's not current. Every January, change the copyright year of the website (if this isn't automatic on your platform) and make all other necessary quantitative updates (e.g., years in business).

Key Takeaways

Here's a quick summary of the key takeaways from Step 5:

- Clients expect freelancers to have a website.

- A clear, compelling website shows clients that you're the right choice. Your "Home" page—the most important part of your website—needs to clearly describe what you do and who you do it for.

- Compelling web content is conversational and concise, focuses on client needs, and conveys key messages quickly.

- Hire a web designer if you want a professional website, unless you're a designer or have very strong design and tech skills.

- Most general advice about websites isn't applicable to freelancers, and some of it can damage your reputation:

  o Don't use images unless they help convey key messages.

  o You don't need a blog.

  o Never use a contact form.

  o Don't worry about SEO.

In Step 6, you'll learn how to meet people who can help and hire you and how to build a strong network.

Step 6. Meet People Who Can Help and Hire You

"If people like you they'll listen to you, but if they trust you they'll do business with you.'

— Zig Ziglar

Succeed by Growing Your Network

Who you know—a.k.a. your network—can be more important than anything else in getting high-paying clients and building a steady, high-income freelance business.

In Step 6, you'll learn how to:

- Get more referrals
- Make key contacts fast by volunteering
- Make the right impression by giving more than you take
- Network effectively in person and online
- Network strategically, especially with colleagues.

Tap Into the #1 Way to Get High-Paying Clients

Word of mouth, a.k.a. referrals, is really powerful. In *How Freelancers Market their Services: 2017 Survey*, freelancers said that word of mouth was the #1 source of their best clients. Other surveys of freelancers and other small business owners have shown similar results. (*How Freelancers Market their Services: 2017 Survey* was a joint venture between The Mighty Marketer, Marketing Mentor Ilise Benun, freelancer Deborah Gordon, MS, and The Accidental Medical Writer.)

Freelancers get referrals from satisfied clients and colleagues. When you do great work, clients will start to refer you to their colleagues, within their organization and at other organizations. So we're going to focus here on getting referrals from colleagues.

Get More Referrals the Easy Way

Networking through professional associations is the fastest and easiest way to build a strong network of colleagues—and get more referrals. It's also a great way to meet clients.

But you only get referrals from colleagues by showing them that you're trustworthy and competent. Doing this takes more than casual interaction.

The Power of Volunteering

Volunteering is the quickest way to build trust and strong relationships and show your competence. When you volunteer, you often meet—and have the chance to impress—leaders in the association. Leaders have large networks.

Most of my new business has come from referrals from colleagues in my main professional association, the American Medical Writers Association (AMWA). This didn't happen by accident. I started volunteering with AMWA the year I joined, both in my chapter and for the national organization. At first, I did small things, like sitting at the registration desk at a chapter meeting and writing articles for our newsletter. Over time, I started presenting at the annual conference and other conferences, served on my chapter's board, volunteered for committees with the national organization, and more.

All professional associations use volunteers, and often you can do something that will help you build skills along with visibility. Look for information on volunteering on each association's website. If you don't see a way to volunteer, email one of the officers.

Give More Than You Take

Helping others without expecting anything in return—or giving more than you take—is the best way to build strong relationships with colleagues and new clients, and to get more business from clients.

Giving more than you take—in person and online—boosts credibility and builds trust. The people you help will remember you when they have a freelance opportunity or something else to share. It's also easier to ask someone for help in the future if you've helped her or him in the past.

And giving makes networking easier. Instead of worrying about selling your services (which is NOT the purpose of networking), you focus on getting to know people by listening to them.

Evidence that Giving Drives Success

Adam Grant, a management professor at the University of Pennsylvania, showed why helping others drives success in his best-selling book, *Give and Take* (2013). Grant found that people who share their time, knowledge, ideas, and connections with others without expecting anything in return ("givers") are more successful than people who focus only on self-promotion ("takers").

Why Takers Lose

Takers are obvious and annoying. When someone I just met asks me for referrals to clients or to work with me as a subcontractor, that's a real turnoff. I never refer work to or hire people unless I know them well and trust them.

Asking for information when you first meet someone is fine. And it's okay to mention the type of work you're looking for and ask whether the person you're talking to knows of organizations that hire freelancers for this. But never blatantly ask someone you don't know well for a referral or a subcontract.

How to Give More Than You Take

It's easy to give more than you take:

*   In person: At networking events, conferences, etc.
*   Online: Through LinkedIn and Twitter, and other online communities for freelancers

- Through email.

We'll cover in-person and online networking in more detail later in this chapter.

Listen when you talk to people in person or communicate with them online. Ask about their work and their interests. Then follow up by sharing information and resources and connecting them to people who may be useful to them. For example, introduce people who do similar work or introduce clients to other types of freelancers they need. Sharing freelance opportunities that aren't right for you is another great way to build your network.

Network Strategically

While you should be nice to everyone you meet, be strategic about how you spend most of your networking time. Figure out which people can be most useful to you, and you to them, and then spend more time and effort building relationships with these key colleagues. Your key colleagues should include other freelancers in your field, as well as freelancers in other fields and full-time employees in your field.

BONUS CONTENT:

Referral Network Form Template

Get more referrals from other freelancers by using this form to start a referral network.

How Freelancers Market their Services: 2017 Survey: Results Report

Learn what works best for freelancers in getting great clients.

https://mightymarketer.lpages.co/bonus-content/

In-Person Networking

Nothing beats in-person networking. Meeting someone in person makes it much easier to build a strong relationship, even if most of your interaction after you meet is through email and social networking. Sometimes you might "meet" someone online, and then develop a strong relationship after you see each other in person.

Meetings, conferences, and other events of professional associations are the best place to meet colleagues. Your associations' annual conferences or other national meetings are a great way to meet many people in a few days. There are also meetings for freelancers you could attend.

Remember, everyone goes to meetings to network and to learn. And most freelancers are shy. Don't be afraid to go up to people and start conversations. Most people will be glad you did.

When networking in person:

- Bring lots of business cards
- Set a realistic goal, like having good conversations with a few people at one event
- Listen for ways you can help the other person
- Ask people questions about themselves
- Be pleasant and professional
- Don't spend too much time with one person.

Make notes on the back of each person's business card so you remember where you met and what you discussed. Follow up with each person you'd like to stay in touch with by:

- Inviting the person to join your LinkedIn network and/or
- Sending an email to say "nice to meet you."

Include details to remind the person about how and where you met.

Connect with and Engage People on Business Social Media

Social media is a key part of business networking now. It helps you:

- Build your network and make key contacts
- Establish yourself as an authority
- Stay in touch with prospects and colleagues
- Learn things that will help you grow your business.

But you must be strategic, or you'll waste a lot of time on social media without getting much in return.

Best Practices in Business Social Media

Always be professional. Be yourself, but behave professionally. Don't do anything on social media that you wouldn't want a client or colleague to see.

Here are a few more best practices when using social media for business:

- Engage people by sharing, commenting, and liking (sharing and commenting are far better than liking)
- Be timely
- Be authentic
- Use images to increase engagement.

The Best Social Media for Freelancers

LinkedIn is by far the most common social network used by freelancers. According to *How Freelancers Market their Services: 2017 Survey*:

- 95% of freelancers who use social networks for business use LinkedIn
- 51% of freelancers who use LinkedIn say it's "important" or "very important" in helping them get clients.

Twitter is the next most common business social network for freelancers. But only 37% of freelancers use it.

I focus mostly on LinkedIn here, with some information about Twitter. If you help clients manage their social networks, then you probably need to use other social networks too, and be more active on social networks than most freelancers.

LinkedIn

Now that you've got (or are working on) a client-focused LinkedIn profile (Step 4), you need to:

- Make contacts
- Build relationships
- Share and engage people.

As mentioned earlier, LinkedIn made many changes in 2017. Under the new interface, more clients will find you on LinkedIn if you have a large network and are active (sharing and engaging). (This information is accurate as of August 2017.)

Build Your LinkedIn Connections
In building your LinkedIn network, focus on quality, not quantity. While a big network is important, it's only helpful if the right people are part of it. Connect with people you know and people you're "related to": people in your industry(ies), other freelancers, etc.

When you invite people to join your network, always send a personal invitation. LinkedIn has made it much easier to do this. Before you had to have the person's email address to send a personal invitation. Now when you want to connect with someone, LinkedIn suggests that you send a personal invitation and lets you click a button to do this.

But beware of "People You May Know," LinkedIn's prompt to invite people to connect with you. If you click on Connect under the person's name and title, LinkedIn sends the automatic invitation. So if you see someone you want to connect with under "People You May Know," search for the person.

When you click on his/her profile, you'll be able to access the box where you can send a personal invitation.

Join relevant groups to get access to many more clients and colleagues. While LinkedIn seems to be trying to hide groups and most groups aren't very active anymore, joining groups lets you connect with other group members, at least for now. Look for the groups that your target clients and colleagues belong to and join the groups that seem most relevant to you.

To find relevant groups:

- Go to the black bar at the top of your LinkedIn home page
- Click on the menu item that says "Work"
- Click "Groups."

Engage People
LinkedIn's new interface makes it easier to engage your network by sharing articles and updates. Sharing and engaging helps you rank higher in search results.

The top of your home page has a prompt to "Share an article, photo, or update." Share relevant articles and updates that people can engage with (like, comment, or share). Most of what you share should be non-promotional. For example, I like to share blog posts, reports, and podcasts about what it takes to succeed in business and ways to be more productive. Sharing the latest news or issues in your industry(ies) is also great.

Once in a while it's okay to mention your own work. But you should always give people something valuable (e.g., a link to something you wrote, the conference where you're presenting, or a related study or other resource).

Don't share only a photo unless it's an infographic. A photo alone has no value to the people in your network and isn't appropriate in business social networking.

Increase engagement by responding to every comment that people make on your posts.

Write Relevant Articles
Writing articles for LinkedIn's easy-to-use, blog-like publishing platform, now called inPUBLISHING (formerly called Pulse) is another way to engage your network. When you publish an article, it becomes part of your LinkedIn profile. LinkedIn shares it with your connections and followers in their news feeds, and sometimes through notifications. If a client finds you by doing a search on LinkedIn, he/she is likely to read your articles, or at least look at the headlines.

"Share your professional expertise," says LinkedIn. "Write about challenges you've faced, opportunities you've seized, or important trends in your industry."

Make sure your articles are relevant to your target clients and colleagues. Think about topics that you know well that they might need or want to know more about. For example, two of my posts from early 2017 are:

- "Do You have the Success Superpower?," about how grit is more important than brains in your success
- "Navigating the New LinkedIn," which I published after LinkedIn made massive changes and everyone was confused.

Write informally but professionally. Don't be overly promotional. Add an image at the beginning of your post.

What You Probably Don't Want to Do on LinkedIn
Everyone talks about—and many gurus recommend—social selling. Social selling involves a series of contacts to build relationships over time, most of which focus on providing your connections with valuable information and resources.

The company doing the social selling develops the resources to show how it can meet the client's needs. For example, say that a technology consulting company sells XYZ technology and trains people in using it. The company might send LinkedIn prospects in the financial services industry a white paper or case study about how XYZ technology helps financial services companies save money.

Social selling is harder for freelancers than for most other businesses. It takes a lot more time and work to do this than to attract clients with direct email (Step 3).

And social selling can only work if your prospects are active on LinkedIn. Otherwise, they're not likely to respond at all. Few clients in my field, freelance medical writing, are active on LinkedIn. They use it when they're searching for free-lancers, but most aren't on LinkedIn regularly. It's probably the same for many other clients.

If you really want to try social selling on LinkedIn and are willing to put a lot of time into this and other marketing, give it a try. Write a top-notch article that's relevant to your target prospects for inPUBLISHING. As part of your social selling, send your prospects a brief description of and the link to the article.

Twitter

I consider Twitter optional for most freelancers. On the plus side, Twitter lets you:

- Build your network
- Learn useful stuff.

On the negative side, you:

- Probably won't get any clients through Twitter
- Can easily waste a lot of time on Twitter.

Of the 37% of freelancers who use Twitter (as per *How Freelancers Market their Services: 2017 Survey*), only 11% rated Twitter as "important" or "very important" in helping them get clients. If you decide to use Twitter, be strategic.

Focus most of your tweets on giving your followers useful information.

My tweets for my freelance business usually offer brief highlights of a study or news item, with a link to more information. I tweet about things that are relevant to my colleagues and clients, but choose things I'm interested in so I learn too, like how to succeed in business and ways to be more productive. As a medical writer, I also tweet health news.

To get more engagement with your tweets include:
- Photos, images, or videos
- Links.

Here are a few more tips on using Twitter:
- Use a service like Buffer to automate your tweets.
- Use lists to organize the people you want to follow.
- Re-tweet other people's best tweets to build relationships.
- Reply to followers who comment on your tweets.

Key Takeaways

Here's a quick summary of the key takeaways from Step 6:

- Word of mouth, a.k.a. referrals from satisfied clients and colleagues, is the best way to get high-paying clients and build a steady, high-income freelance business.

- Networking through professional associations is the fastest and easiest way to get more referrals, and volunteering is the quickest way to build relationships that lead to referrals.

- Giving more than you take is the best way to build relationships and grow your business.

- Nothing beats in-person networking for building strong relationships.

- LinkedIn is by far the most common social network used by freelancers; 51% of freelancers who use LinkedIn say it's "important" or "very important" in helping them get clients.

In Step 7, you'll learn how to stay in touch with interested clients who haven't yet hired you (and current clients) and colleagues so they think of you first when they need a freelancer or have freelance work to refer.

Step 7. Be First in Line for Freelance Work

"The ladder of success is best climbed by stepping on the rungs of opportunity."

— *Ayn Rand*

Succeed by Creating Top-of-Mind Awareness

Up to 90% of the time, prospects aren't ready to hire a freelancer when you first contact them, according to business coach and strategist Ed Gandia. And 80% of sales (in general, not specific to freelancing) are made after at least five marketing contacts, according to Entrepreneur, HubSpot, and others.

In Step 7, you'll learn how to:

- Get high-paying clients by making sure that:
    - Clients think of you first when they're looking to hire a freelancer
    - Colleagues think of you first when they have work to refer.

- Stay in touch with colleagues and interested clients without actively "selling yourself." Interested clients have expressed interest in your services but haven't hired you yet.

- Develop a list of your interested, current, and inactive clients, and colleagues and a plan for targeted follow up—so you can get more high-paying clients.

Use Targeted Follow Up

Many freelancers miss getting great clients because they never or rarely follow up with clients who've expressed interest in their services but haven't hired them. The single most important thing you can do to get great clients is to stay in touch with these interested clients regularly, so that you'll be first in line for freelance work.

Sometimes, it takes a year or more of following up to get a client. One of my best clients hired me nearly two years after I first started marketing to him. We've been working together since 1999. It's also important to stay in touch with clients you haven't worked with for a while and colleagues, who are a great source of referrals.

By following up regularly, you create that all-important top-of-mind awareness. This is a fancy way of saying that you'll be first in line when clients need a freelancer or colleagues have work to refer. I call this targeted follow up.

Be Helpful, Relevant, and Persistent

Targeted follow up isn't hard. And it isn't about "selling yourself." In fact, most of the time, you shouldn't even mention your freelance services. Targeted follow up is about being relevant, helpful, and persistent. Once you get organized, it only takes a few minutes every now and then.

Customized Follow Up: The Best Type

Most of your follow up should be customized to the client or colleague, because this makes more of an impression. For clients, an easy way to do this is to comment on news, blog posts, etc., about your contact person or the organization. Ways to find news include:

- The company's Newsroom page
- Google Alerts
- LinkedIn updates or tweets.

For example, when one of my interested clients hired a new CEO, I sent my contact a LinkedIn message saying that I hoped this was good news for her, along with a link to the story. I found out about this because I subscribe to the client's e-newsletter. Reading the story and sending the message took about two minutes. When my contact replied, she was impressed that I knew about the new CEO.

Share Relevant Resources

You can also share relevant resources from reputable individuals or organizations, like:

- Reports
- Podcasts
- Industry updates
- Free software
- Other free tools.

Sometimes you can use the same resource for multiple people, but you'll be sending it to them one at a time, so it will look like it's customized to each person.

Develop a library of resources so you won't have to scramble to find relevant resources and information when it's time for your next follow up:

- Sign up for e-newsletters that are relevant to your clients and colleagues

- Look for resources in relevant LinkedIn updates and tweets (I get lots of great resources to send clients and colleagues through social media)

- Check out resources from your professional associations and industry organizations or publications.

There's a lot of great free content on the web these days that you can use for targeted follow up. Here are just a few sources:

- SmartBriefs: E-mail news summaries and other content in more than a dozen areas, including business, finance and healthcare, with subtopics for each

- Social Media Examiner: An e-newsletter and links to many reports, blogs, and podcasts about social media

- Pew Research Center: Surveys and reports on many topics, including business, Internet, and healthcare

- Entrepreneur.com: Articles on all aspects of running a business and e-newsletters (geared toward entrepreneurs, but many articles have widespread relevance).

Keep a folder with these resources (or links to them). If something is very timely, like my interested client's new CEO, send it along right away. Otherwise, tuck it away for your next scheduled follow up. You can also use these resources for your LinkedIn updates (and tweets if you use Twitter).

Generic Follow Up

Generic targeted follow up is where you send the same thing to everybody on your list, like holiday cards or your e-newsletter. Sending holiday cards—print cards that arrive in the mail—is another way to help people remember you, especially if you get them out early. Mine are in the mail the Monday after Thanksgiving weekend.

Developing your own e-newsletter is a great way to follow up with clients and colleagues. Most of the content should be useful information and resources.

An e-newsletter also lets you highlight your expertise and interests. For example, I love doing content marketing for hospitals and other healthcare clients, and featured how these clients can use digital channels to attract more patients in a recent issue of my e-newsletter.

Direct Email Follow Up

Once or twice a year, it's fine to send a gentle direct email reminder that you're available for freelance work to:

- Interested clients
- Inactive clients (clients you haven't worked with for a while).

Email to Interested Clients

Send a professional, low-key email. Write a subject line with a reminder about your original direct email, like:

> Following up on [date] email about helping XYZ Hospital attract more patients

> or:

> Checking in to see whether I can help ABC Company meet freelance writing needs

After reminding the client about his/her response to your original direct email, use information from that direct email to highlight how you can help the client meet its needs. End with your call to action and contact information.

Email to Inactive Clients

Something as simple as a friendly greeting followed by "miss working with you and XYZ Company and would love to work with you again" can be effective.

Email as Part of Follow Up

But direct email follow up must be part of your overall follow up. It should never be the only time you contact interested and inactive clients.

Organize and Commit to Targeted Follow Up

Your targeted follow-up list should include:

- Interested, current, and inactive clients

- Key colleagues (the people you think will be most useful to you, and you to them, especially other freelancers)

- The 20-30 prospects you most want to work with (your hot prospect clients).

Schedule Your Targeted Follow Up

Once you have your list, put targeted follow up on your calendar—and treat it like a deadline for a client. Block out:

- 30-60 minutes a week to look for news and review resources for your resources library
- 2-4 hours a month for following up with people (depending on how many people are on your list).

Here's what I recommend for your follow-up schedule:

- Interested clients:
  o About every 2 months

- Hot prospect clients:
  o 1-2 weeks after your initial marketing contact and then about every 3-4 months

- Current and inactive clients:
  o About every 3 months

- Key colleagues:
  o About every 3-4 months

BONUS CONTENT:

Targeted Follow-Up Tracking Template

An easy way to schedule and track your follow up

https://mightymarketer.lpages.co/bonus-content/

Review Your Targeted Follow Up

At least once a year, review your targeted follow-up list. Many experts recommend staying in touch with people for about two years. If you haven't received any response from an interested or inactive client after that, you could take the person off your list.

But there are many stories about freelancers who got a high-paying client after years of follow up. In fact, in 2016, this happened to me. Four years earlier, one of my clients moved to another organization. After that, I sent her my e-newsletter and holiday cards. Occasionally, I commented on something she posted on LinkedIn. In 2016, she hired me for a freelance job that was so big that I had to bring in three other freelancers to work with me.

So if you really want to work with a particular client who hasn't responded to your targeted follow up, it may be worthwhile to keep that client on your list.

Add new interested clients, new clients, new hot prospects, and new colleagues to your follow-up list whenever you get or meet them. Keep all clients on your targeted follow-up list.

Key Takeaways

Here's a quick summary of the key takeaways from Step 7:

- Up to 90% of the time, prospects aren't ready to hire a freelancer when you first contact them.

- Be first in line for high-paying freelance work by staying in touch with interested, current, and inactive clients, and colleagues regularly.

- Stay in touch mostly by giving people relevant information and resources.

- Make time for targeted follow up. Put this on your calendar and treat it like it's a deadline for a client.

Next, I'll share with you my journey as a freelancer.

After my story, check out the list of Bonus Content for Your Freelance Success I've put together for you.

My Mistakes and My Journey to Freelance Success

"I am a great believer in luck.
The harder I work, the more I have of it."
— *Thomas Jefferson*

Succeed by Learning from Others

Like most freelancers, I knew very little about running a business when I quit my job and became a full-time freelancer in 1997. Looking back at all of the mistakes I made, it's just embarrassing. But I'm going to be brave and share some of them with you here.

My Biggest Mistakes

My two biggest mistakes were not having a strong specialty and not knowing enough about my target clients. I made other mistakes too, like not knowing how to network strategically and not following up enough.

Not Specializing Enough or Knowing My Target Clients

In Step 1, I told you about how I started out as a freelance medical writer. That's a specialty, and a great one, but it was too broad. In the beginning, I thought that freelance medical writers were all like me, people with journalism degrees who wrote about health, healthcare, and medicine. And I thought they all did marketing communications, like I did.

I was wrong! Most medical writers (freelance or employed) have medical or scientific degrees. Most freelance medical writing isn't marketing communications. It's more scientific writing, which I'm not qualified for or interested in doing. I learned all of this after I joined the American Medical Writers Association.

But before that, I had been marketing to many companies that would never hire me—because they use freelance medical writers with medical or scientific degrees for projects that I call "high science."

Despite this, I was able to build my freelance business to 6 figures in 18 months—because I did a massive amount of marketing. And I adjusted my marketing as I learned more about my target clients and freelance opportunities in medical writing (remember, this was 1997, when the web was in its infancy and I couldn't research clients and opportunities online).

Not Networking Strategically

I always knew that networking was important. So I joined the American Medical Writers Association the year I started my business and volunteered right away. I've been an active member ever since.

But I treated everyone I met the same way. It took me years to realize that I needed to be more strategic about networking. Since I was very active, I was able to build a strong network quickly anyway. But I could have built a more relevant network much more quickly if I had been strategic. Now, I spend most of my networking time and effort on people who are most likely to be key contacts for me and me for them.

Not Following Up Enough

The first 18 months or so, while I was actively building my business, I did a massive amount of marketing and followed up regularly with interested clients. But as I got busier and busier, I followed up less and less.

Later, at various times in my freelance career when I lost clients (for reasons unrelated to my work) and I needed to market actively again, I regretted not following up more. It took me more time and effort to find, research, and attract new clients than it would have taken me to follow up with those interested clients, some of whom would probably have become my clients.

My Journey to Freelance Success

Succeeding as a freelancer isn't easy. We all make mistakes. But as my story shows, you can still succeed even if you make a lot of mistakes.

Two things helped me succeed despite my mistakes:

- Determination
- Hard work.

When I started my business, I bought a silver cup engraved with the quote from Jefferson that I used at the beginning of this chapter:

> "I am a great believer in luck. The harder I work, the more I have of it."

I put that cup on my desk where I saw it every time I looked up from my computer.

Over the years, I've met hundreds of other freelancers, and I've realized that those of us who succeed aren't luckier or smarter than freelancers who struggle. We are determined to succeed, and we are willing to do the work.

There is no such thing as overnight success. It takes time—and effort—to build a successful freelance business.

My Confession

I do have a confession to make: I love marketing. Yes, I know; I'm weird! But even if you don't know what to do or think you hate marketing, you can do it. Marketing is just another skill, and skills can be learned.

Let me give you an example. Public speaking is a skill that I had to force myself to learn. As a kid, I was so shy that I used to hide behind my mom when people came to see us, even people I knew well. The first time I gave a presentation, I felt like I was going to faint and I held onto the podium with a death grip the entire time.

Then, I studied public speaking and I practiced. Now I enjoy giving presentations. If I can learn to be comfortable as a public speaker, you can learn how to be a Mighty Marketer.

Hope is Not a Strategy

There's a simple truth behind freelance success: If you want high-paying clients who treat you right and give you steady work, you've got to go out and get them—through marketing. Then you have to do great work so they keep hiring you.

Hope is not a strategy. Great clients don't just fall into your lap—unless you've set the stage with your marketing.

Saying Yes when Opportunity Knocks

Everything you do and everyone you meet can lead to freelance opportunities. I became a freelance medical writer by agreeing to proofread a supermarket's employee news-letter for a printing company. Sound boring? It was.

But proofreading that newsletter got me a big client in medical editing and a steady income when I quit my job and launched my full-time freelance business a few years later.

One day, my client called and asked if I would be interested in copyediting a journal on drug and device development. Although I'm a writer and not an editor, I said yes. And my client referred me to his client, a non-profit association for professionals working in medical product development.

I spent the next 10 years copyediting the journal, eventually also doing some writing for the association. This was my introduction to the lucrative and interesting field of medical writing and editing.

The First 18 Months

During my first 18 months as a full-time freelancer, in 1997 and 1998, I aggressively marketed my business. I developed a business name, a logo, and a tagline and used them in pro-fesssional marketing materials: business cards, brochures, stationery, envelopes, and direct mail pieces. I didn't have a website because the web was in its infancy.

I joined the American Medical Writers Association to learn more about the medical writing marketplace and to network. And I started volunteering right away.

It was a lot harder and more expensive to launch a freelance business back then, because I didn't have all of the web-based resources that freelancers today have. I had to go to the library to develop my prospect lists and use direct mail instead of direct email to attract clients. In those first 18 months, I sent 3 direct mail flyers to about 250 prospects each. This cost me about $7,000. But it was the foundation of my success.

At the end of those 18 months, I was making 6 figures. My biggest worry was how to keep up with all of the work.

I learned two key lessons that I teach other freelancers today:

- **You have to follow up:** A few clients contacted me within days of receiving my first flyer. But most hired me after receiving the second or third flyer. One client hired me about two years after I sent him the first flyer—and we've been working together since 1999.

- **Referrals are the easiest way to get new clients, and networking is the best way to get referrals**: Volunteering for the American Medical Writers Association, and focusing my networking on helping others without expecting anything in return, led to lots of referrals. I never asked for these referrals; back then I was too shy to do this. But the people who got to know me trusted me and sent opportunities my way.

My Freelance Business Over the Years

In 2002, as the web was starting to grow, I developed my first website. At the time, few freelancers had websites. I was also an early adopter of social networking for business, joining LinkedIn back in 2004, the year after it was established.

Like all freelancers, I've lost clients, including some very big clients. Here are a few of my stories:

- When a new editor at a client I loved, and had been working with for years, revised everything I wrote so that it was full of mistakes, I fired the client. I did try to resolve these issues but was unable to do so.

- After a top hospital hired me to write web content, things went well until they hired a new marketing manager who wanted a lot more content than specified in the contract. I agreed to expand the project, but said that this would result in a significant increase in the cost. The project manager said no. Was it any surprise that the new marketing manager didn't like my work and the client never hired me again?

- Most recently, I lost my biggest client when they just decided to stop doing the work that I had been doing for them for 18 years.

I have more stories like this. But I'm sure that you get the point: Bad things happen to all freelancers.

When these things happened to me, I did feel sorry for myself—at first. But I knew that a pity party wasn't going to do me any good. So I ramped up my marketing.

Within a few months, I always had new clients—and usually more work than I really wanted.

Losing or firing clients also gave me an opportunity to think about my business and where I wanted to take it. I targeted my marketing to the type of work I most wanted to do for the types of clients I most wanted to work with. And I ended up doing more of what I liked best.

BONUS CONTENT:
SMART Goal Worksheet
Set and achieve your goals and use mini-goals to make steady progress.

Freelance Medical Writing and Editing: A High-Income, High-Demand Specialty
Learn more about what medical writers and editors do and whether this could be the right specialty for you.

https://mightymarketer.lpages.co/bonus-content/

Key Takeaways

YOU TOO CAN BECOME A MIGHTY MARKETER

Getting the clients you deserve and building a steady, high-income freelance business isn't as hard as you probably think it is (as long as you're competent in your freelance field). You really only need three things:

1. Knowledge
2. Determination
3. Hard work.

In this book, I've showed you what to do and how to do it (the knowledge part). It's up to you to add the determination to succeed and to put in the work.

Every freelancer can become a Mighty Marketer.

Bonus Content for
Your Freelance Success

"If you're smart enough to be a freelancer,
you're smart enough to be a Mighty Marketer."

— *Lori De Milto*

Templates, Checklists, Worksheets, and More

Use the bonus content to help you succeed in freelancing.

GET ALL BONUS CONTENT:

https://mightymarketer.lpages.co/bonus-content/

(NOTE: After mightymarketer, the next letter is "l" as in lion).

Reading the paperback?

For an electronic link to the bonus content, just email themightymarketer@comcast.net and write Bonus Link in the subject line.

Bonus Content

Step 1:

The Absolute Best Way to Attract Bigger, Better Clients

Step 2:

Prospect List Template

Step 3:
Direct Email Swipe File

Step 4:
LinkedIn Profile Checklist for Freelancers

Step 5:
Freelance Website Checklist

Step 6:
Referral Network Form Template

How Freelancers Market their Services: 2017 Survey: Results Report

Step 7:
Targeted Follow-up Tracking Template

My Mistakes and My Journey:
SMART Goal Worksheet

Freelance Medical Writing and Editing: A High-Income, High-Demand Specialty

Made in the USA
Columbia, SC
24 May 2018